RECORDER FUN!™

THE BEATLES

CONTENTS

Cover photo: Val Wilmer / Contributor / Getty Images

ISBN 978-1-4950-6278-0

7777 W. BLUEMOUND RD. P.O. BOX 13819 MILWAUKEE, WI 53213

E-Z Play Today® Music Notation © 1975 by HAL LEONARD CORPORATION
E-Z PLAY and EASY ELECTRONIC KEYBOARD MUSIC are registered trademarks of HAL LEONARD CORPORATION.

Visit Hal Leonard Online at
www.HalLeonard.com

GETTING STARTED

HOLDING THE RECORDER

Here is how to hold the recorder. The mouthpiece rests on your lower lip, just like a drinking straw, with only a little of it actually going inside your mouth. Be sure that all of the finger holes line up on the front of the recorder as shown in the picture.

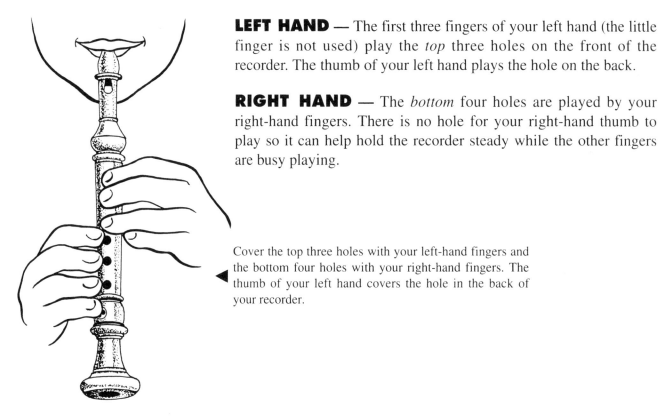

LEFT HAND — The first three fingers of your left hand (the little finger is not used) play the *top* three holes on the front of the recorder. The thumb of your left hand plays the hole on the back.

RIGHT HAND — The *bottom* four holes are played by your right-hand fingers. There is no hole for your right-hand thumb to play so it can help hold the recorder steady while the other fingers are busy playing.

Cover the top three holes with your left-hand fingers and the bottom four holes with your right-hand fingers. The thumb of your left hand covers the hole in the back of your recorder.

MAKING A SOUND

To make a sound on the recorder blow gently into the small opening at the top of the mouthpiece. You can change this sound by covering different holes with your thumb and fingers. For example, when you cover all of the thumb and finger holes you will get a low, quiet sound. When only one or two holes are covered the sound will be higher and much louder.

Here are some tips for getting the best possible sound out of your recorder:

Always blow gently into the mouthpiece — Breathe in and then gently blow into the mouthpiece as if you were sighing or using a straw to blow out a candle. Remember, always blow gently.

Leaks cause squeaks — Play the holes using the pads of your fingers and thumb (not the tips). Press against each hole firmly so that it is completely covered and no air can sneak out. Even a tiny leak of air will change a beautiful tone into a sudden squeak!

Use your tongue to start each tone — Place your tongue against the roof of your mouth just behind your front teeth and start each tone that you play by tonguing the syllable "du" or "too" as you blow gently into the recorder.

PLAYING A TONE

Musical sounds are called *tones*. Every tone has a letter name. *Finger charts* are used to show you exactly which holes should be covered in order to play a particular tone. Each circle on these charts represents one of the holes on your recorder. The thumb hole is represented by the circle to the left of the recorder in the chart.

●   means that you should cover that hole.

○   means that that hole should not be covered but left open.

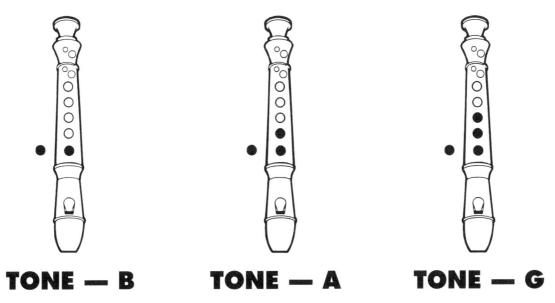

TONE — B   TONE — A   TONE — G

Use these three tones to play "Mary Had A Little Lamb:"

MARY HAD A LITTLE LAMB

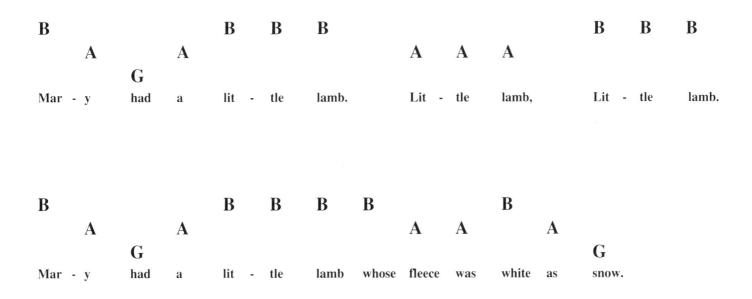

B			B	B	B				B	B	B
	A		A			A	A	A			
		G									
Mar - y	had	a	lit - tle	lamb.	Lit - tle	lamb,	Lit - tle	lamb.

B			B	B	B	B			B		
	A		A				A	A	A		
		G								G	
Mar - y	had	a	lit - tle	lamb	whose	fleece	was	white	as	snow.

READING MUSIC

Musical notes are an easy way to see everything that you need to know in order to play a song on your recorder:

How high or low — Notes are written on five lines that are called a *staff*. The higher a note is written on the staff the higher it will sound.

How long or short — The color of a note (black or white) tells you if it should be played short or long. The black notes in "Mary Had A Little Lamb" are all one beat long (*quarter notes*). The first three white notes in this song are two beats long (*half notes*) and the last note is four beats long (*whole note*).

How the beats are grouped — The two numbers at the beginning of the song (4/4) are called a *time signature*. This time signature tells you that the *beats* in this song are grouped in fours: **1** 2 3 4 **1** 2 3 4 etc. To help you see this grouping, *bar lines* are drawn across the staff to mark each *measure* of four beats. A *double bar* is used to mark the end of the song.

Now here is how "Mary Had A Little Lamb" looks when it is written in musical notes:

MARY HAD A LITTLE LAMB

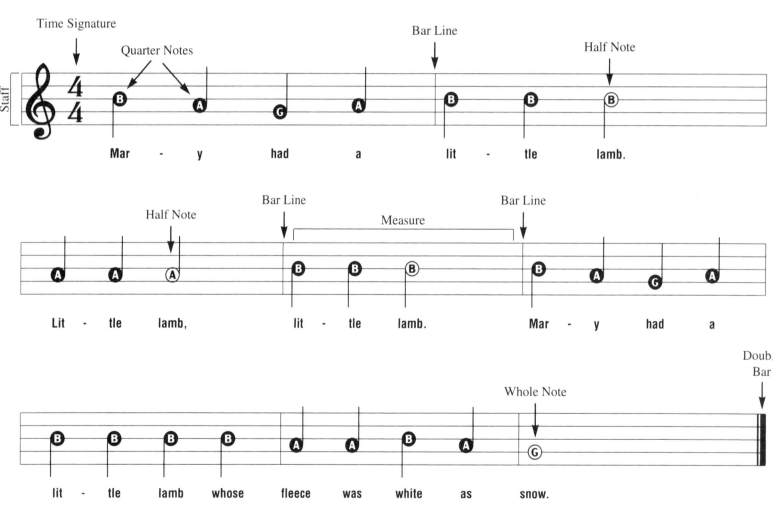

TWO NEW TONES

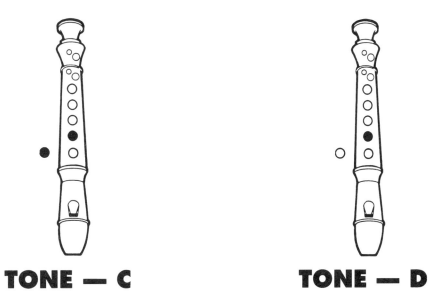

TONE — C   **TONE — D**

AURA LEE

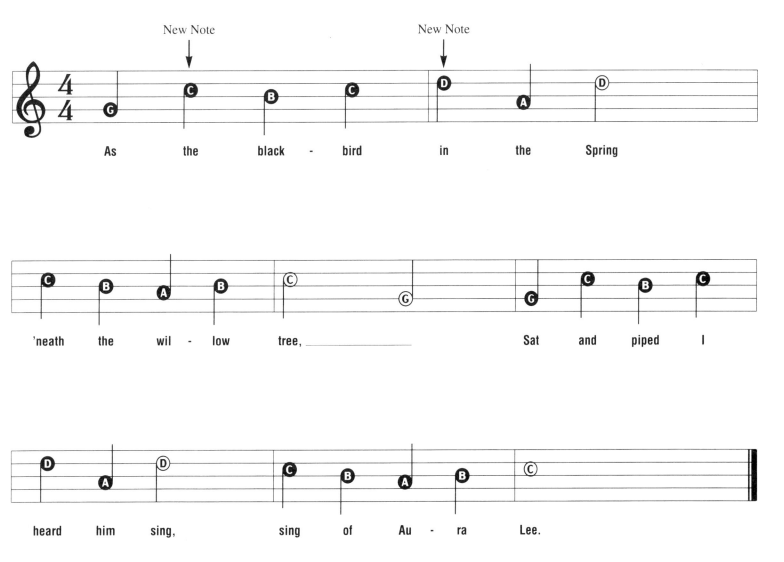

USING YOUR RIGHT HAND

"Twinkle, Twinkle Little Star" uses the tone E. As you can see from the fingering chart, you will use three fingers of your left hand and two fingers of your right to play this tone. The thumb hole is only half filled in (◑). This means that you should "pinch" the hole with your thumb so that only a small part of the hole is left open. Pinching is done by bending your thumb so that the thumbnail points directly into the recorder leaving the top of the thumb hole open.

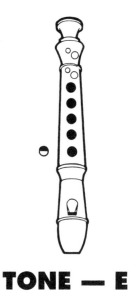

TONE — E

TWINKLE, TWINKLE LITTLE STAR

NOTES AND RESTS

In addition to notes that are one, two or four beats long, other values are possible. Also, *rests* are used to indicate when you should *not* play a tone but be silent. The chart on page 7 will help you identify the different notes and rests that are used in this book.

COUNT:

	1	&	2	&	3	&	4	&	NUMBER OF BEATS	REST
WHOLE NOTES	o								4	—
HALF NOTES	♩				♩				2	—
QUARTER NOTES	♩		♩		♩		♩		1	𝄽
EIGHTH NOTES	♫		♫	(or)	♫		♪ ♪		1/2	𝄾
& SIXTEENTHS	♬		♬	(or)	♬		♬♬		1/4	𝄿

DOTTED NOTES ARE 1 1/2 TIMES THE NORMAL LENGTH:

	1	&	2	&	3	&	4	&
DOTTED-HALF & QUARTER	♩.						♩	
DOTTED-QUARTER & EIGHTHS	♩.			♪	♩.			♪
DOTTED-EIGHTHS & SIXTEENTHS	♪. ♬		♪. ♬		♪. ♬		♪. ♬	

TRIPLETS ARE SPREAD EVENLY ACROSS THE BEATS:

	1	&	a	2	&	a	3	&	a	4	&	a
QUATER-NOTE TRIPLETS		3						3				
EIGHTH-NOTE TRIPLETS		3			3			3			3	

THIS OLD MAN

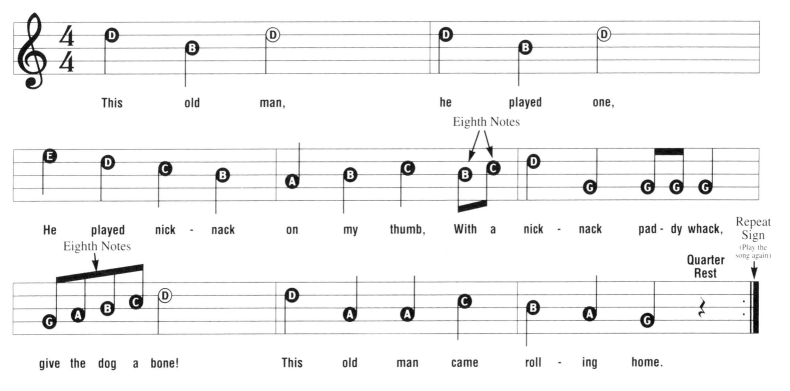

FINGERING CHART

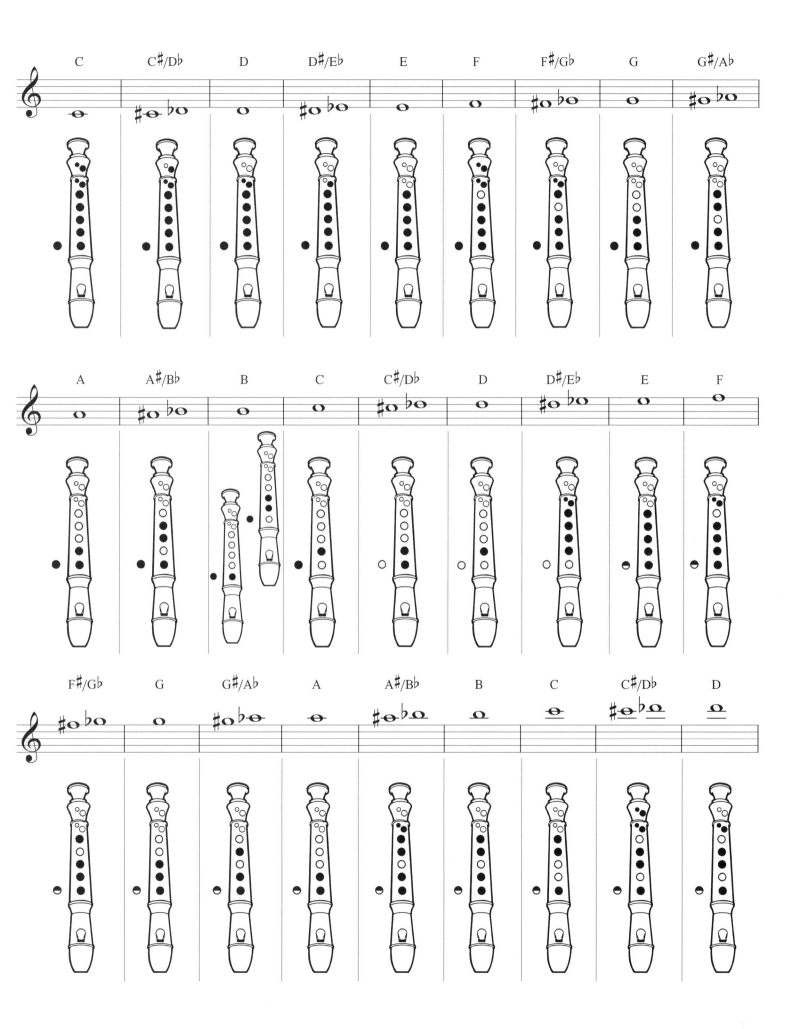

ALL MY LOVING

Words and Music by John Lennon
and Paul McCartney

GET BACK

Words and Music by John Lennon
and Paul McCartney

I FEEL FINE

Words and Music by John Lennon
and Paul McCartney

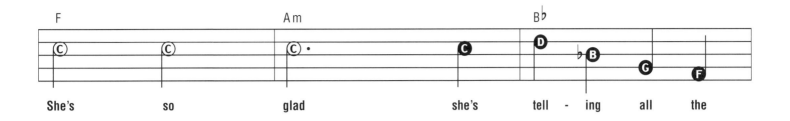

F · · · Am · · Bb

She's so glad she's tell - ing all the

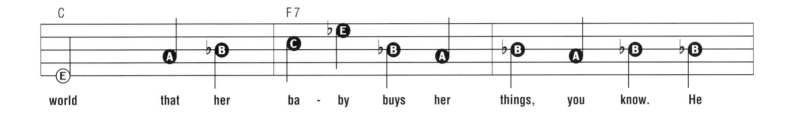

C · · F7 · · · C

world that her ba - by buys her things, you know. He

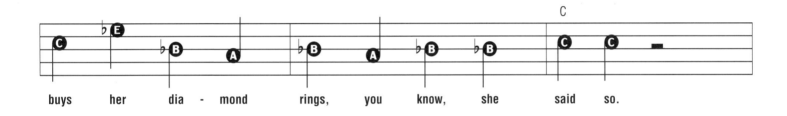

buys her dia - mond rings, you know, she said so.

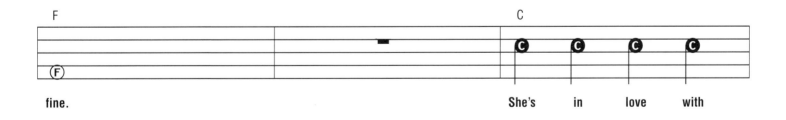

Bb

She's in love with me and I feel____

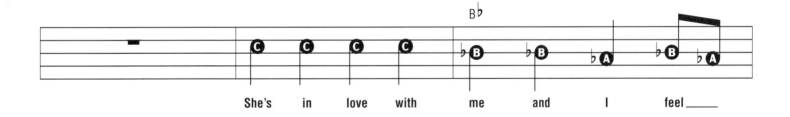

F · · C

fine. She's in love with

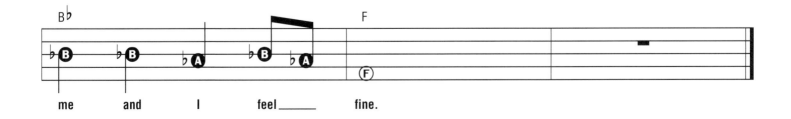

Bb · · F

me and I feel____ fine.

LADY MADONNA

Words and Music by John Lennon
and Paul McCartney

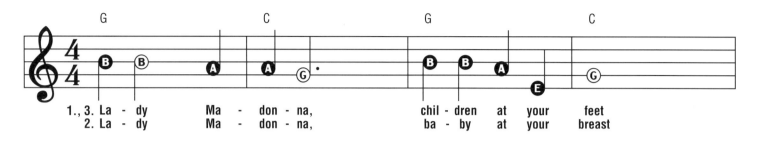

1., 3. La - dy Ma - don - na,   chil - dren at your feet
2. La - dy Ma - don - na,   ba - by at your breast

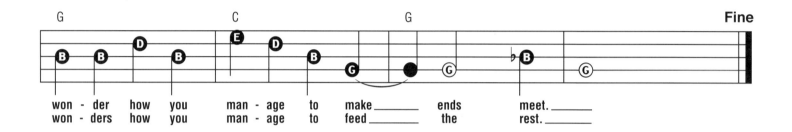

Fine

won - der how you man - age to make _____ ends meet. _____
won - ders how you man - age to feed _____ the rest. _____

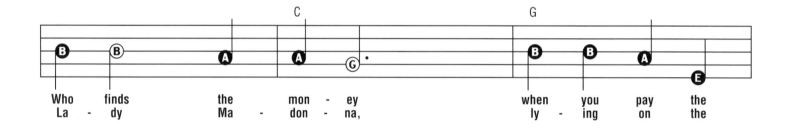

Who finds the mon - ey   when you pay the
La - dy Ma - don - na,   ly - ing on the

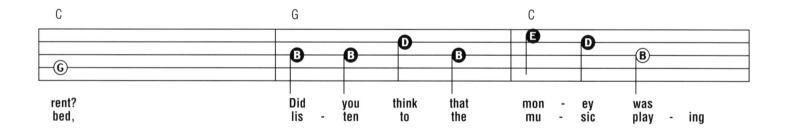

rent?   Did you think that the mon - ey was
bed,   lis - ten to the mu - sic play - ing

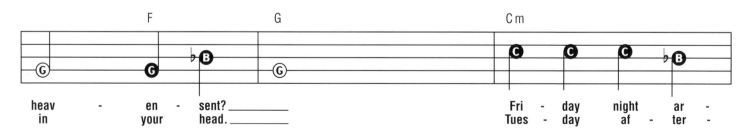

heav - en - sent? _____   Fri - day night ar -
in your head. _____   Tues - day af - ter -

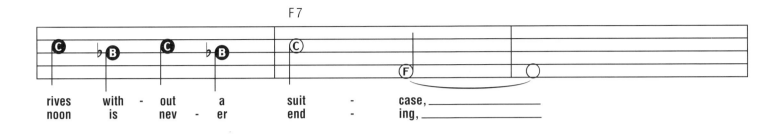

rives with - out a suit - case,_____
noon is nev - er end - ing,_____

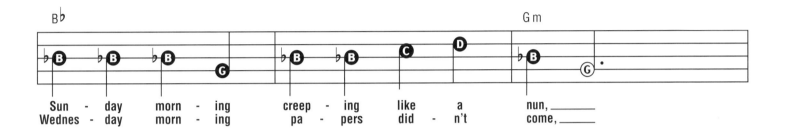

Sun - day morn - ing creep - ing like a nun,_____
Wednes - day morn - ing pa - pers did - n't come,_____

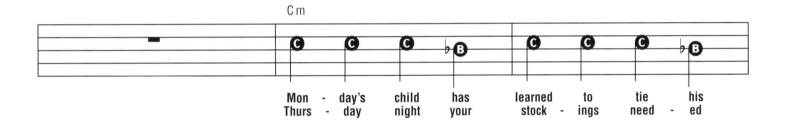

Mon - day's child has learned to tie his
Thurs - day night your stock - ings need - ed

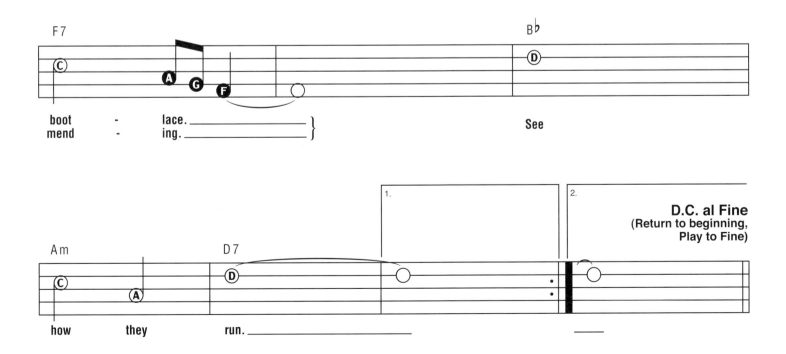

boot - lace._____ }   See
mend - ing._____

1.

2.

D.C. al Fine
(Return to beginning,
Play to Fine)

how they run._____

NOWHERE MAN

Words and Music by John Lennon
and Paul McCartney

17

SHE LOVES YOU

Words and Music by John Lennon
and Paul McCartney

B♭m

loves you, and you know you should be glad.

C7

To Coda ⊕

1.

She Ooh.

2.

She

Dm

loves you, yeh, yeh, yeh. She loves you, yeh, yeh, yeh. And with a

G7

D.S. al Coda
(Return to ℅
Play to ⊕ and
Skip to Coda)

B♭m

love like that, you know you should be glad. ____

C7

F

You

CODA
⊕

Ooh. She loves you, yeh, yeh, yeh. She loves you, yeh,

Dm

G7

yeh, yeh. And with a love like that, you know you should be glad. ____

B♭m

C7

F

And with a love like that, you know you should be glad. ____

B♭m

C7

F

YELLOW SUBMARINE

Words and Music by John Lennon
and Paul McCartney

Yesterday

Words and Music by John Lennon
and Paul McCartney